T0334774

THE LITTLE
SPRINGTIME
BOOK OF
GNOMES

THE LITTLE
SPRINGTIME
BOOK OF
GNOMES

KIRSTEN SEVIG

THE COUNTRYMAN PRESS
A Division of W. W. Norton & Company
Independent Publishers Since 1923

Copyright © 2021 by Kirsten Sevig

Photo on page 6 by Jennifer Jang Helgesen

All rights reserved
Printed in the United States of America

For information about permission to reproduce selections
from this book, write to Permissions, The Countryman Press,
500 Fifth Avenue, New York, NY 10110

For information about special discounts for bulk purchases,
please contact W. W. Norton Special Sales at
specialsales@wwnorton.com or 800-233-4830

Library of Congress Cataloging-in-Publication Data

Names: Sevig, Kirsten, author, illustrator.
Title: The little springtime book of gnomes / Kirsten Sevig.
Description: First edition. | New York, NY : The Countryman Press,
a division of W. W. Norton & Company, [2021]
Identifiers: LCCN 2020054788 | ISBN 9781682684801 (hardcover) |
ISBN 9781682684818 (epub)
Subjects: LCSH: Gnomes. | Gardening. | Seasonal cooking. | Spring—
Meditations. | Spring—Folklore. | Folklore—Norway.
Classification: LCC GR549 .S479 2021 | DDC 398.209481—dc23
LC record available at https://lccn.loc.gov/2020054788

Manufacturing by Versa Press

The Countryman Press
www.countrymanpress.com

A division of W. W. Norton & Company, Inc.
500 Fifth Avenue, New York, NY 10110
www.wwnorton.com

10 9 8 7 6 5 4 3 2 1

To Huckleberry,
who has brought me
so much joy,
and who made
completing this book
nearly impossible!

Hello, lovelies!

My name is Kirsten Sevig and I am an artist from Minnesota, currently living in Vermont. In order to understand how this book came to be, you must first know that my family is very Norwegian. One could go so far as to say *extremt norsk*. My sister and I were raised in the only Norwegian-speaking household on the block, often listening to the great Nordic folktales that feature many gnomes. I have loved gnomes ever since, so imagine my delight when I learned that a lesser-known word for proverb is:

gnome /nōm/
noun
noun: **gnome**; plural noun: **gnomes**

1. a legendary dwarfish creature who wears a pointed hat.

2. a wise, pithy saying; maxim.

Of course, I couldn't resist combining the two, so here we are. This book is a celebration of gnomes and one of my favorite seasons: springtime! Days grow longer, birds return, animals awaken, and tiny buds burst open in the most brilliant shade of green. Because spring is a great time to make a fresh start, I decided that my gnome world should be more colorful, inclusive, and reflective of what that traditional folklore would look like when reimagined for today.

In these pages, you will find gnomes busy with their springtime activities: cleaning, gardening, climbing trees, and picking strawberries—all while showering us with the great wisdom that only gnomes can bestow! You'll also find some of my favorite springtime crafts and recipes to try along the way. So don a daisy crown and explore the colorful springtime world of gnomes!

Hjertelig hilsen,

No matter how long the winter,
spring is sure to follow.

What is hidden in snow
is revealed at thaw.

One gnome's trash
is another gnome's treasure.

Nothing is so bad
it isn't good for something.

Life begins the day
you start a garden.

Plant kindness,
gather love.

Water the seeds
you want to grow.

Sprouting Seeds

Both delicious and nutritious, sprouting may just become your new favorite pastime! Eat them by the handful or enjoy with any meal.

Materials:

- a wide-mouthed mason jar
- 3 tablespoons sprouting seeds
- a sprouting lid (or cheesecloth)
- a bowl

Instructions:

1. Place the seeds in a clean jar, cover with cool water, and gently swirl. Let the seeds soak for 8 hours, then drain.

2. Rinse the seeds with cool water twice, swirling the seeds before draining. In a warm room (about 70°F), invert the jar into a bowl at a 45° angle, out of direct light.

3. Repeat step 2 for 4 to 6 days. Empty the bowl as needed.

4. Most seeds sprout within a day or two, but they can be eaten at any stage. When you are ready to harvest, place the jar in direct sunlight for a few hours to allow the sprouts to turn green. Cover and refrigerate any uneaten sprouts and consume within a week. Enjoy!

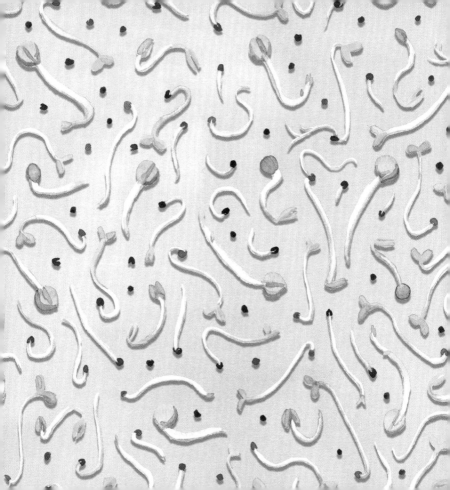

A prudent gnome doesn't
make a goat their gardener.

A bad gardener
quarrels with his rake.

Butterflies forget that
they were once caterpillars.

To an optimist,
every weed is a flower.

One gnome's weeds
are another gnome's supper.

Dandelion Pesto

Makes 1 jar of pesto

*I was so pleasantly surprised by how much I loved this somewhat bitter pesto.
Be sure to harvest your dandelion leaves where no chemicals have been sprayed.*

Ingredients:

- 2 cups packed dandelion leaves, cleaned and chemical-free
- ½ cup walnuts (or substitute almonds or pecans)
- 6 garlic cloves, unpeeled
- ½ cup freshly grated Parmesan cheese (or nutritional yeast)
- ½ cup extra virgin olive oil
- ½ teaspoon salt
- Ground black pepper to taste
- Juice of ½ lemon

Instructions:

1. In a frying pan over medium-high heat, lightly brown
   the unpeeled garlic cloves until soft, about 10 minutes.
   Peel the cloves when cooled.

2. In the same pan over low heat, toast the walnuts
   for 3 to 5 minutes or until lightly browned. Set aside.

3. In a food processor, combine the dandelion leaves, garlic, walnuts, and salt. Stop to scrape down the sides of the bowl until everything is incorporated.

4. Pulse while drizzling in the olive oil until you reach your desired consistency.

5. Add the Parmesan cheese (or nutritional yeast) and lemon juice and pulse. Season to taste.

6. Refrigerate the pesto in an airtight container and use within a week, or freeze to enjoy for much longer.

A new broom sweeps clean,
but the old broom knows
the dirty corners best.

Stairs should be swept
starting at the top.

A tree must be climbed
from the bottom.

Don't saw off the branch
you are sitting on.

Blooming Branches

Enjoy the beauty of spring by watching branches come to life in your own home. It is magic!

Materials:

- branches with plump buds
- a clean, sharp knife
- a hammer
- a narrow-necked vase, bottle, jar

Instructions

1. In late winter/early spring, select branches that are at least 12 inches long with several big, tight buds on them from trees or shrubs that will flower. I love forsythia!

2. Cut them away at the base of the stem using a clean sharp knife. Trim away any parts that aren't to your liking.

3. Cut the stem at an angle and hit the base with a hammer a few times before arranging in a vase with warm water.

4. Once you have arranged the branches to your liking, place them somewhere with bright, indirect light that is between 50 and 70°F. For best reuslts, give them fresh water and trim and hammer the base every few days. Most branches will bloom between 1 and 8 weeks.

Ducks quack louder
before the rain.

Sometimes it snows in April.

A baby's bottom
and April weather
cannot be trusted.

Every path has its puddle.

A little puddle
can make a big splash.

Jump in with both feet.

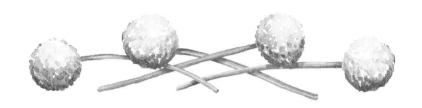

April showers
bring May flowers.

Actions speak
louder than words.

Good things come in threes.

Empty pots make
the most noise.

Don't cross the stream
to find water.

Don't throw away
the old bucket until
you know the new one
holds water.

She who finds a stone
to rest on will be relieved…

twice.*

* Once when sitting down and once when standing up again.

Good things come
to those who forage.

Every bird
loves their nest.

Away is good…

but home is best.

Slow and steady
wins the race.

The simplest things
can be the sweetest.

Strawberry Rhubarb Crisp

Serves 4

*This recipe is easy to make and can be adjusted to suit your needs.
I make it gluten-free and vegan.*

Fruit Ingredients:

- 2½ cups strawberries, halved
- 2½ cups rhubarb, diced
- 2 tablespoons organic sugar
- 1 tablespoon cornstarch
- 1 teaspoon cinnamon

Crisp Ingredients:

- 1 cup rolled oats
- ½ cup almond flour
- ½ cup raw walnuts, chopped
- ¼ cup light brown sugar
- 1 pinch of sea salt
- 4 tablespoons butter or oil

Instructions:

1. Preheat the oven to 350°F. Grease an 8-inch square baking dish.

2. In a medium bowl, combine the fruit ingredients until evenly coated and place in the greased baking dish.

3. Combine the crisp ingredients in a bowl, adding the butter or oil last, and spread evenly over the fruit. Bake for 40 minutes. Serve with vanilla ice cream.

A good friend
is like a four-leaf clover:
hard to find
and lucky to have.

Joy can be found in searching.

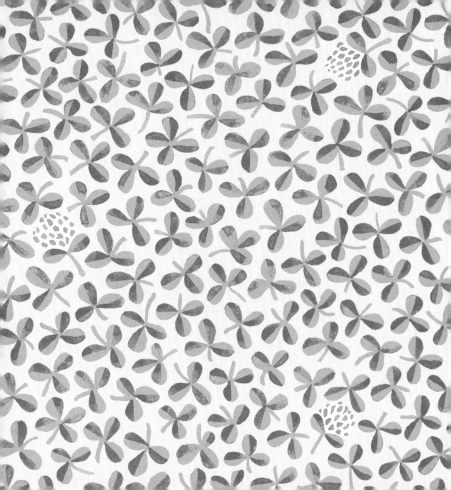

Don't put all your lilacs
in one basket.

Lilac Syrup

Makes 1 ½ cups

To give your favorite drinks a springtime flavor, try making this simple syrup infused with lilacs! Try lilac lemonade, lilac iced tea, and lilac cocktails or mocktails!

Ingredients:

- 1 cup sugar
- 1 cup water
- 2-4 cups fresh lilac florets, clean and chemical-free
- 1-2 blackberries (optional, for color)

Instructions:

1. Place the sugar and water in a saucepan over medium heat. Simmer until the sugar dissolves. Remove from the heat.

2. Stir in the lilac florets and blackberries, if using. Cover, allowing the lilac florets to infuse for 2 hours (or longer for more intense flavor).

3. Pour through a fine-mesh sieve, possibly twice, to strain out any pieces of lilac. Then pour the syrup into a jar and refrigerate. Use within 1 month for the best flavor.

A heart in love with beauty
never grows old.

A book is a garden
you can carry in your pocket.

Remember to stop
and smell the flowers.

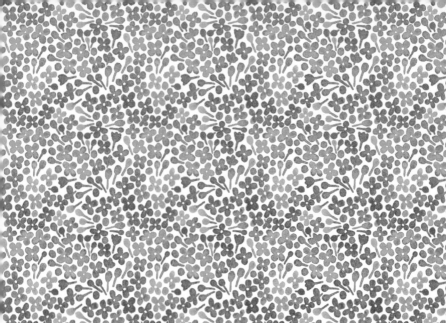